When the Pasture is Not an Option

Preparing for Retirement

TERRY PILE

When the Pasture is Not an Option:
Preparing for Retirement

Copyright

Cover and interior design: Laura O'Brien

Reproduction

Table of Contents

INTRODUCTION
It's Not All About Money

"Your vision will become clear only when you can look into your own heart. Who looks outside, dreams. Who looks inside, awakens."
—Carl Jung

The average American spends 90,000 hours working toward retirement and less than ten hours planning for it. And most of that planning is financial. Financial well-being, however, is only one third of the retirement formula. Physical and emotional well-being also fit into the retirement equation. There is plenty of literature on how to prosper and stay healthy. Finding happiness, however, is more elusive.

Many individuals who are in the habit of going to work every day find the hardest part of being retired is filling their days with meaningful activity. A full-time job provides very little time for developing interests and relationships outside of work. Those who have developed a special hobby or interest, often find it isn't enough to get them through the typical workweek.

Taking the time for self-assessment and reflection are the first necessary steps to discovering the activities that might be emotionally fulfilling. Knowing what options are available is important, too. Conducting research and exploring your options are the next practical steps to help you clarify your vision. Finally, developing an action plan is your roadmap to realizing your dreams.

How to use this book

Planning a path to retirement is not unlike planning a career path. Through self-assessment, values analysis, options research and strategic planning, this book will help you develop an action plan to assist you in your transition to a productive and fulfilling life after work. **Tip:** Keep a print or digital notebook handy. Use it to record the exercises, observations and other ideas that may pop-up as you work through this Quick Study Guide.

CHAPTER I

Identifying Your Interests:
Take a Trip Down Memory Lane

"You have to put off being young until you can retire."

- Author unknown

They say youth is wasted on the young. Perhaps it is just put on hold until retirement. Youth was a time for exploring the world around us--participating in sports, playing an instrument, joining after school clubs, or simply "hanging out" with friends. During youth, we had the time and the opportunities to partake in hobbies and interests that helped develop our character and intellect. Then we grew up. Work and family obligations dominated. If there was any "free time" left for special interests, it was minimal.

Retirement is your second chance. It is an opportunity to rekindle youthful interests. This time around, you can explore the world with purpose and appreciate what a luxury it is to devote your time and energy to activities you really love.

Perhaps you have forgotten what those interests were, or maybe you would like to explore new options. The following exercise is a trip down memory lane. It will help you identify enjoyable activities from your past and translate them into potential retirement avocations.

EXERCISE

Identifying Enjoyable Experiences

There are three steps to this exercise.

1. Search your memory as far back as you can for moments of enjoyment or pleasure. These memories can come from childhood, school, work, family/friends and volunteer activities.
2. Identify what it was about these experiences that brought you enjoyment.

3. Look for clues to identify new experiences you may want to research and consider trying.

EXAMPLE

1. Describe your enjoyable experience.

Playing chess with your friends in a backyard tent on a rainy day.

2. What are the elements that made this experience pleasurable?

Being with friends. Being out in nature. Using strategy. Element of competition.

3. List possible new opportunities to research and consider.

A. Join or form a weekly chess group.

B. Learn to play bridge or another strategy game.

C. Consider joining a hiking club or make hiking dates with friends or family members who share in the enjoyment of nature.

Now you try it. On a sheet of paper or notebook, come up with six enjoyable experiences and then brainstorm with yourself or someone close to you about the possibilities. Use the format below:

1. Describe your enjoyable experience.

2. What are the elements that made this moment pleasurable?

3. List possible new opportunities to research and consider.

If you are having trouble coming up with enjoyable experiences, don't despair. The following exercises in the Quick Study Guide should help you dig deeper into your reservoir of positive memories.

CHAPTER II

Identifying Your Skills and Abilities: Exploring Proud Moments

"If people concentrated on the really important things in life, there'd be a shortage of fishing poles."

—Doug Larson

The enjoyable experiences exercise should have conjured many positive emotions. Perhaps it prompted you to make a list of former hobbies and activities you would like to revisit. For some, having a few pleasurable activities is all that is required for a fulfilling retirement. Others want to be involved in more challenging endeavors using the skills and abilities they have honed after years of being in the workforce. Those who seek such challenges often turn to volunteer work or reenter the workforce in a part-time or consultant capacity because these are venues where their strengths can be put to good use.

Maybe you have never taken the time to think about what it is you are really good at and enjoy doing. By analyzing your "proud moments," you will discover a great deal about your skills and abilities. You will often find patterns in these stories and discover that many of the strengths and abilities you enjoy you have been using since childhood. Career counselors call these dependable strengths. Because you enjoy using them and undoubtedly do them well, you will want to consider incorporating them into your retirement life.

EXERCISE

Identifying Your Dependable Strengths (Skills and Abilities)

This exercise has four steps:

1. Think about the things you have done in your private or public life that you enjoyed doing, did well, and made you feel proud. For example, it could be teaching your puppy to do tricks, helping a customer solve a problem, winning an award, finding an

accounting error that saved your company money or offering a suggestion that increased productivity. Try to come up with six proud moments (personal and professional) and tell your story using the format provided. You may want to include and expand upon some of your enjoyable experiences you described in the exercise in the previous chapter. Give each "proud moment" a one or two word title so you can identify it for future exercises and incorporate some background information.

2. Explain the action(s) you took.

3. Describe the results.

4. At the end of each story, identify the skills and abilities required to accomplish the task.

EXAMPLE

Name of Proud Moment:

Joke Book

Background:

When I was in 5th grade, elephant jokes were all the rage. They went something like this...

Question: "How can you tell if there is an elephant in your refrigerator?"

Answer: "Look for footprints in the Jell-O."

Yes, they were silly, but I loved hearing, telling and collecting them.

Actions:

When I had collected about 50 elephant jokes, I decided to "publish" them. I spent a couple Saturday's in my father's office typing the jokes up, drawing a cover, photocopying the pages and producing 25 booklets. I sold them to friends and classmates at school for ten cents. I made a total of $2.50. I enjoyed the process of collecting jokes, writing and editing them, producing the books and making sales.

Results:

I published my first book and made lots of people laugh. It felt great to know that others appreciated my efforts. Also, $2.50 was a reasonable profit for a fifth grader in those days, which made me feel successful.

Skills and Abilities:

Artistic/Creative, Marketing/Promotion, Production, Research, Sales, Writing/Editing, Articulate, Business-

minded, Imaginative, Industrious, Persuasive, Self-motivated

Now you try it. Write several proud moments on another sheet of paper or in a notebook, using the format below. It is recommended that you strive for a minimum of six stories to reveal patterns in the skills and abilities you have used in the past.

Name of Proud Moment:

Background:

Actions:

Results:

Skills and Abilities:

Once you have completed your proud moments go back and look for patterns or themes. Are there skills and abilities that appear over and over? Do your stories share any similarities such as organizing events, teaching or training others, creating innovative ways to do things more simply? Document your observations regarding patterns and themes in your notebook.

In the next chapter, you will consider how to combine your dependable strengths (skills and abilities) with your values to create meaningful retirement activities.

CHAPTER III

Identifying Your Values: What's Really Important?

"The harder you work, the harder it is to surrender."
—Vince Lombardi

Too often we are so busy living life, we forget to slow down and consider what it is that makes life satisfying and meaningful. Retirement is an opportunity to explore the values we hold dear By clarifying your values or belief systems, you will have established guidelines that will help you decided how you can employ your skills and abilities to get the greatest satisfaction out of that period of life we call retirement.

EXERCISE

Identifying Your Values

Below is a list of commonly held beliefs or values.
Read and rate each value according to the following 1-
4 scale:

4 = very important

3 = somewhat important

2 = less important

1 = not important

If you have a value that is important to you but is not
on the list, add it at the bottom and rate it.

Values List	4	3	2	1
Appreciation of beauty/nature				
Optimism for the future				
Relationships with family/friends				
Playfulness				
Spirituality				
Creativity/originality/ingenuity				
Open-mindedness				
Love of learning				
Teaching/counseling others				
Generosity/Altruism				
Financial gain/Success				
Citizenship-social responsibility				
Fairness-giving others a chance				

Leadership

Integrity

Industriousness

Forgiveness and mercy

Gratitude

Honesty

Vitality

Humility

Immortality—leaving a legacy

Physical challenge

Competition

Physical health

Mental health

_____

_____

Go back to your list of values and look at the 4's, the values most important to you. Then rank the 4's in order of priority. List your top five values in your notebook.

CHAPTER IV

Researching Your Options

"Half our life is spent trying to find something to do with the time we have rushed through life trying to save."
—Will Rogers

By analyzing your enjoyable experiences and proud moments, you may have uncovered information about yourself that you had forgotten or never knew existed. Perhaps themes such as teaching others or solving complex problems jumped out at you.

Now it is time to do some research on the options you may want to use to combine your dependable strengths with your values to create meaningful activities. These options include:

- Recreation and Hobbies
- Volunteering

- Continuing Education
- Employment (full or part-time)
- Self-employment

Recreation and Hobbies

Retirement is a time to indulge in the things that really interest you. It may be traveling, collecting, artistic expression, inventing or participating in physical activity. You can choose to do it alone or with others. Every hobby or recreational activity has its own lexicon, rules and culture. You can dive in deep or skim the surface.

Resources to help you with your research include:
Discover A Hobby - www.discoverahobby.com
HobbyLark - www.hobbylark.com
Your local Parks & Recreation website
Your local Community College

Volunteering

Volunteering is a wonderful way to apply your experiences and dependable strengths for the common good. Many organizations would not exist without volunteers, and retirees overwhelmingly dominate this group. Pick a cause you care about. The choices are many: the arts, children, the elderly, human rights, the homeless, the environment, animals, diseases, education, politics....

Resources for exploring volunteer opportunities include:
Volunteer Match - www.volunteermatch.org
Volunteers of America - www.voa.org
Volunteer Abroad - www.volunteerabroad.com

Continuing Education

Most students cannot wait to get out of school. Many adults cannot wait to get back in. It isn't uncommon to hear about people in their sixties, seventies, eighties and older returning to school to complete studies that were interrupted or to earn a new degree.

Are you interested in learning a foreign language, improving your computer skills trying your hand at creative writing, taking up an instrument, studying philosophy or the world's religions? Whatever your interest, there is a class for the life-long learner that dwells within.

Your local library or the Internet can assist you in finding these educational resources:

Local universities and community colleges certificate and extension programs

Department of Parks and Recreation continuing education programs

Online universities and institutes

Special interest groups—seminars and workshops

Study abroad programs

Lifetime Learning Centers

Employment

Being retired does not mean you can never go back to work. If you miss the camaraderie around the water cooler or you are a natural born workaholic, consider part-time, seasonal or contract (project based) work. If you loved what you did or where you worked, look for a need and create a proposal describing how you would fill it. Create your own job description then approach your former employer or an employer you would like to work for and show the benefit you can bring to the organization.

Some popular career options for retirees who want to return to work include:

Adjunct Professor

Accountant or Bookkeeper

Chauffeur or Taxi Driver

Customer Service Representative

Dog Walker or Groomer

Event Planner

Fundraiser

Holiday Sales Clerk (seasonal)

Hotel Front Desk Clerk

IT Help Desk Associate

Patient Advocate

Sales Associate

Sales Demonstrator

Security Guard

Store Greeter

Tax Preparer

Tutor

Resources to consider if you are thinking of returning
to the workplace include

American Association for Retired Persons (AARP) -
www.aarp.org

Senior Job Bank - www.seniorjobbank.org

Workforce 50 - www.workforce50.com

Indeed - www.indeed.com

Self-Employment

Perhaps you miss working but don't miss having a boss. Consider self-employment. Being in business for yourself can take many forms. You can become a freelancer, a consultant working independently, or affiliate with a group. You can buy a franchise or someone else's business. Starting an online business holds all kinds of possibilities for the entrepreneurial spirit. Remember, going into business can be risky and is a tremendous time commitment. Do plenty of soul searching and research before you jump in.

Resources to get you started include:
Small Business Administration - www.sba.gov
Franchise Association- www.franchiseba.com
The Story Exchange – www.thestoryexchange.org
(women entrepreneurs)
Freelance.com - www.freelance.com
Upwork.com - www.upwork.com
Virtual Vocations - www.virtualvocations.com

Important Issues to Consider

Your research can be invigorating and discouraging at the same time. It is exciting to see all the options laid out before you and to know you now have the time to actually pursue them. It can be discouraging as well, because you can't do it all or you may have a hard time deciding which you want to do most.

As you begin developing your action plan in the next chapter, ask yourself the following:

How much time do you want to commit to this activity?

Many retirees will say, "I am so busy, I don't know how I got everything done when I was working." Part of this busyness comes from a reluctance to say "no" and over committing one's time. Once you retire, people assume you have extra time on your hands. All of a sudden, you are called on to babysit the grandkids, check on your neighbor's dogs, participate in church activities and a myriad of other requests. Pick your activities carefully, keeping in mind family obligations and protecting your time for the things that mean the most to you.

Can I afford the financial commitment?

When most people retire, they are on a fixed income. Engaging in expensive hobbies or investing in a business that could jeopardize your financial security is neither realistic nor wise. Again, make sure you do your research.

Am I healthy enough and do I have the physical stamina required?

Your mind and heart may have the desire to climb mountains, but consider the risks involved to your body. Today's older adults are in better shape and more physically active than ever before. If you are going to consider new activities that require physical stamina, check with your doctor first, and join a training program to get you into the right shape for the sport you have selected.

How will this activity impact my relationship with family and friends?

Out of sight, out of mind frequently applies to retirement. It is difficult not to make friends or establish relationships when you are going to school or working at a job. When you are retired and out of circulation, it is easier for former co-workers and professional colleagues to forget about you. If all your friendships are connected to the workplace, consider activities that will include old friends or give you the opportunity to establish new friendships. Either way, it will be up to you to take the initiative.

The most important dynamic to consider when you begin reshaping your new life, is your relationship with family members. Being retired will naturally have an impact on your relationships either good or bad. Include those you care about in your decision making as you explore new activities. Is your partner supportive? Does he or she feel left out? Have you included activities that you can do together? Your decisions can enhance close relationships or do serious damage.

EXERCISE

List other issues you need to consider in your notebook.

CHAPTER V

Putting It All Together

"You don't get to choose how you're going to die, or when. You can only decide how you are going to live. Now."
—Joan Baez

You've analyzed your enjoyable experiences, proud moments and options for retirement activities. You have also given some thought to those special considerations: health, time, money and relationships. Now it is time to pull all your research together.

EXERCISE
Putting It All Together

Draw from the activities you listed in your notebook to complete this exercise.

1. Prioritize the activities you are considering from most likely to least and list them on the left side of the chart.

2. At the top of each column, list the skills, abilities and values that are most important to you.

3. Then list any important issues you identified in the previous chapter that you need to consider.

4. Next rate each activities as it relates to the skills, abilities, values and considerations on a 1 – 4 scale with 4 being highly probable and 1 being least probable.

5. Total the rows.
You will be able to see at a glance which activities best meet your criteria for a fulfilling retirement.

6. Based on your *Putting It All Together* analysis you have completed, reprioritize the top three to five activities you want to consider.

EXERCISE

Sample Retirement Options Analysis

Ranking Options with Priorities

(Use scale from 1-4 with 1 being least optimal and 4 most optimal)

EXAMPLE

Sample Retirement Options Analysis

Option	Priority 1	Priority 2	Priority 3	Priority 4	Total
	Hands on	Involves animals	Flexible hours	Minimal financial risk	
Animal Shelter Volunteer	4	4	3	4	15
Start a dog walking business	4	4	1	2	11

Your Retirement Options Analysis

Option	Priority 1	Priority 2	Priority 3	Priority 4	Total

CHAPTER VI
Moving Ahead

"The trouble with retirement is that you never get a day off."

—Abe Lemons

Being retired means waking up every day to a new adventure. The best part is that you are in control of what the adventure will be. It is an enviable position to be in, and an opportunity you don't want to squander. You have done the groundwork. Now you need to develop the roadmap to get you to your destination.

EXERCISE
Developing a Retirement Action Plan

In this exercise, you will develop a Retirement Action Plan. The Plan will help you determine the next steps you need to take to make your retirement successful.

Look at the Retirement Action Plan worksheets below. It is an example to use as a reference.

EXAMPLE

Sample Retirement Action Plan

Activity	Strategy	Next Steps	Concerns	Deadline
Take a memoir writing class	Continuing Education	Check community college catalog or local parks & rec program	Should be less than $50	This winter
Start a chess club for teens	Volunteering	Contact local middle school	Limit to 12 students at first	Early fall

Your Retirement Action Plan

Activity	Strategy	Next Steps	Concerns	Deadline

Whether retirement is just around the corner or a few years from now, you are on the right track to preparing yourself for a meaningful future. Arlene Mandell best sums up the freedom and lightheartedness that she felt in retirement in her poem, *All Dressed Up*.

ALL DRESSED UP

By Arlene L. Mandell

On Retirement: 75 Poems, Edited by Robin Chapman & Judith Strasser, University of Iowa Press

A bit of gel to tame
my springy curls,
a clean T-shirt and shorts,
sandals and sun screen,
most days this is all
I need for the library,
hardware store or
farmers' market.

Switch to white slacks,
add earrings and a squirt
of green tea cologne
and I'm ready for our indie film house
followed by a tasty meal
at bistro or barbecue joint.

Once I wore linen suits,
pantyhose, sling-back pumps
and makeup—foundation,
liner, blush, mascara—

so much time and money
to project that chic
public relations image.
Now retirement is my profession
and I'm out the door in ten minutes.

May your retirement be your profession, filled with
fun, good health, prosperity and all that you hold dear.

SUMMARY
Wrapping Up

Let's review the key points addressed in this Quick Study Guide.

1. A fulfilling retirement requires more than financial planning.

2. Begin thinking about retirement by revisiting enjoyable experiences and proud moments from your past.

3. Identify your skills, abilities and values that are important to you.

4. Consider issues such as relationships, money, physical limitations and time.

5. Create a retirement action plan that will serve as a roadmap to guide you in this new phase of your life.

Next Steps

1. Sit down with your spouse, partner, other family member or friend who you may want to involve or will be impacted by your retirement plans and discuss the exercises completed. Explore how those close to you can be involved in your activities or support you in your pursuits.

2. Make a list of contacts with the people you will want to network with to discuss your retirement activities and how you might go forth in pursuing them. Tap into their resources and knowledge about these activities. Solicit advice and suggestions.

3. If some of the activities you want to pursue are not doable now, revisit them in the future. It is important to revisit your goals and action plan periodically and to make revisions depending on your current situation.

ADDITIONAL RESOURCES
Helpful Links

Age Brilliantly provides a variety of special offers and resources to seniors –
www.agebrilliantly.org

American Association of Retired Persons (AARP) offers numerous books and resources related to retirement planning –
www.aarp.org/retirement

America Volksport Association for walking clubs -
www.ava.org

Area Vibes – calculates the cost of living in a variety of cities
www.areavibes.com/salary-calculator

Bolles, Richard N. and John E. Nelson - *What Color is Your Parachute? For Retirement,* Berkley: Ten Speed Press

Borchard, David C - *The Joy of Retirement,* New York: AMACOM

Chapman, Robin and Judith Strasser (Edited by) - *75 Poems on Retirement* - Iowa City: University of Iowa Press

Collamer, Nancy – *Second-Act Careers: 50+ ways to profit from your passions during semi-retirement,* Berkley: Ten Speed Press

Continuing education by state - www.seniorresource.com/senioreducation.htm

Discover A Hobby - www.discoverahobby.com

Planning for your financial retirement - www.usa.gov/retirement

Toastmasters International for public speaking –

www.toastmasters.org

Volunteer Match –

www.volunteermatch.org

Volunteer Travel Abroad -

www.gooverseas.com/volunteer-abroad/seniors

BONUS ARTICLE

Retirement Undone, by Terry Pile

(Revised and updated in 2017 from original article "Checking out Unretirement" by Terry Pile, printed in The Mercer Island Reporter)

Among the 50-something crowd, conversations often turn to retirement with common themes of spending time with grandchildren, traveling, doing volunteer work and starting new hobbies. But retirement may not be all that it's touted if 44 percent of retirees return to work at some point during their "golden years," as a Cornell University study suggests.

Money is one compelling reason why a retiree may return to work. A lackluster retirement portfolio, unexpected expenses or insufficient savings force many retired Americans to return to the workplace. For Rhonda T., a customer service representative at a local grocery store, it was all about benefits.
"I've been self-employed for most of my working life and didn't have much in the way of retirement benefits," said Rhonda. "I've worked at this grocery

store for seven years now. I have the energy for it and I love working here. I really like the customers and the people I work with."

John G., the grocery store's general manager, says he has at least seven "unretirees'" on his payroll. Many work for the benefits. A 15-hour work week will secure medical benefits, while a 20-hour work week makes employees eligible for family coverage as well. "That adds up to about $6,000 a year," John G. points out. Money isn't the only reason people return to work. Some enjoy the intellectual challenges, companionship or the satisfaction of doing a job well.

For Paul S., the interim superintendent of a suburban school district, returning to work was all about choices. "I take on jobs because I want to, not because I have to," said Paul. "Working as an interim superintendent requires a different talent. You need to know people quickly and take a plan that's not yours and keep it moving. I also like to work with outstanding people. That's fun."

When Dan B. retired from his job as an airplane mechanic, he had no plans to return to work. In fact, he enjoyed his first year of retirement, tinkering around his house as well as doing small repairs for friends and neighbors. "At some point, I realized I could get paid for having fun and I started my own business, Handyman Dan. I choose when I want to work and pick the jobs I want. They usually take less than a week." Dan often gets calls from real estate agents to make minor repairs on a home before it goes on the market. Once the home is sold, the new owner often calls back for additional fixes. Dan recently took on a second job, "taking care of my three grandchildren. The pay is low but it is very satisfying work."

For some, retirement is an avocation. John H., a former engineer, considers retirement his work. "My goal is to enjoy every minute of my day. I always have a queue of things to do like reading, biking, corresponding with family and friends or walking my dog," John said. "I feel like I'm working when I go out on my bike for three or four hours. I put in a hard day working to keep fit."

If you are contemplating "unretirement," here are a few things to think about:

Financial considerations

Going back to work may not necessarily have financial benefits. Figure out how much money you need to earn, after taxes and expenses, to make going back to work worthwhile. Don't forget to include the cost of lunches, commuting and clothing. Since earned income will be added to your current income, you may find yourself in a higher tax bracket. For those ages 62-64, there is a Social Security penalty of $1 for every $2 earned over a certain limit. You may consider not drawing Social Security while you are working, or delay going back to work until you turn 65, when no penalty applies.

The age factor

Although we often hear about age discrimination, most employers still value the maturity, work ethic and experience of the older worker. According to the Five O'clock Club, a national career counseling network, "Older workers represent the talent pool; younger workers are the talent pipeline. The latter depends on the former." Because older workers often worry about age discrimination and stereotyping, the Five O'clock Club suggests the following: pay particular attention to image and attire, appear enthusiastic and energetic, show a willingness to pitch in, even on the smallest jobs, and capitalize on age and experience. Many companies with a young work force want a few gray heads around to deal with important clients and help the company avoid mistakes. Age and experience do count!

Have fun

Confucius said, "Do what you love and you will never have to work." Whether you are repairing cupboards, waiting on customers, or fixing your bike, the work you do should be fun and satisfying. That's the best compensation of all in those "unretirement" years.

About the Author
Terry Pile, GCDF

Terry Pile is a retired Career Counselor/Coach and certified Global Career Development Facilitator (GCDF). She was the founder and principal consultant for Career Advisors. Prior to career counseling, Terry was a public-school teacher and marketing executive. For over 17 years she taught individuals (as diverse as college students, home-makers, CEOs and ex-offenders) how to market themselves to find satisfying employment.

Writing and publishing is Terry's retirement career. She is the author of *Changing Careers After 40: Real Stories, New Callings* in addition to many other inspirational and self-help books. You can find her books and other career resources at www.BiblioPilePress.com or through your favorite bookseller.

Made in the USA
Monee, IL
07 July 2026

56552299R00030